Development Aid
End It or Mend It

Peter Bauer

apx 6438

An International Center for Economic Growth Publication

ICS PRESS
San Francisco, California

Publication of this Occasional Paper was funded by the United States Agency for International Development (AID).

Publication signifies that the International Center for Economic Growth believes a work to be a competent treatment worthy of public consideration. The findings, interpretations, and conclusions of a work are entirely those of the authors and should not be attributed to ICEG, its affiliated organizations, its Board of Overseers, or organizations that support ICEG.

Inquiries, book orders, and catalog requests should be addressed to ICS Press, 720 Market Street, San Francisco, California 94102 USA. Telephone: (415) 981-5353; fax: (415) 986-4878. For book orders and catalog requests, call toll-free in the continental United States: **(800) 326-0263.**

Library of Congress Cataloging-in-Publication Data

Bauer, P. T. (Péter Tamás)
    Development aid : end it or mend it / Peter Bauer.
      p. cm. — (Occasional papers / International Center for Economic Growth ; no. 43)
    Includes bibliographical references.
    ISBN 1-55815-276-8
    1. Economic assistance. I. Series: Occasional papers (International Center for Economic Growth) ; no. 43.
HC60.B323   1993
338.9—dc20   93-8145
                                               CIP

PREFACE

The International Center for Economic Growth is pleased to publish Lord Peter Bauer's *Development Aid: End It or Mend It* as the forty-third in our series of Occasional Papers, which feature reflections on broad policy issues by noted scholars and policy makers.

Lord Bauer is professor emeritus of economics at the London School of Economics and one of the incisive critics of development aid programs. In this paper he analyzes the West's often uncritical commitment to government-to-government development aid, arguing that it is based on several highly suspect assumptions. He clarifies the point that aid is not sufficient or even necessary to lift developing countries out of poverty, and regards as unanswerable the question of whether aid promotes or inhibits economic advance. He questions those who hold that aid is useful to prevent developing nations from posing serious political or security threats to the West. Finally, he critiques the belief that government-to-government aid serves to improve the lot of the poorest people in developing countries. Although Lord Bauer is dubious of the prospects for meaningful reform of the West's aid policy, he offers some suggestions for improving the chances that aid will achieve its proclaimed objectives.

With budget limitations restricting the largess of Western donors, and with the emergence of new governments seeking aid in Eastern Europe and the constituent states of the former Soviet Union, governments are being forced to re-examine their aid policies. In these circumstances, critiques of aid, such as Lord Bauer's, could not be more timely. Efforts to rethink the goals of development aid—realistically—can be enormously abetted by the attention of scholars and policy makers to his insights and observations.

The experience of multilateral international development assistance organizations and some bilateral aid programs has demonstrated that there can be significant transfers not only of financial resources but also of technology, training, institution building and policy advice to devoloping countries. Quite often technology transfer is as useful as financial aid. Prof. Bauer's criticisms and suggestions can be useful to improve on those fruitful experiences as well as to remind us of the challenge of carefully targeting aid programs to help people to develop themselves.

Nicolás Ardito Barletta
General Director
International Center for Economic Growth

December 1993
Panama City, Panama

ABOUT THE AUTHOR

Peter Bauer (Lord Bauer) is professor emeritus of economics, London School of Economics, University of London; fellow of the British Academy; and fellow of Gonville and Caius College, Cambridge. Before becoming professor at the London School of Economics, he held various academic teaching posts at London University and at Cambridge University. He has been visiting professor or visiting lecturer in many universities in Europe, America, Asia, and Africa. He was elevated to the peerage in 1982.

Lord Bauer has published a number of books and many journal articles in applied economics, especially in development economics. His books include *The Rubber Industry* (1948); *West African Trade* (1954, 1963); *The Economics of Underdeveloped Countries* (with B. S. Yamey, 1957); *Economic Analysis and Policy in Underdeveloped Countries* (1958); *Indian Economic Policy and Development* (1961); *Markets, Market Control and Marketing Reform* (with B. S. Yamey, 1968); *Dissent on Development* (1972, 1976); *Equality, the Third World and Economic Delusion* (1981, 1982); and *Reality and Rhetoric: Studies in the Economics of Development* (1984). His most recent book, *The Development Frontier*, was published by Harvard University Press in 1991.

Peter Bauer

Development Aid: End It or Mend It

Since the early years after World War II, subsidies in the form of grants or soft loans from governments of relatively rich countries to those of relatively poor countries have been an accepted component of international relations. This policy is known as foreign aid in the United States and as development aid elsewhere.[1]

The Axiomatic Approach to Aid

These subsidies expanded from a few hundred million U.S. dollars a year in the late 1940s to about fifty billion dollars annually by the 1980s. The multilateral component of these subsidies, negligible in the 1940s, grew to about $20 billion per year by the 1980s. In the early days of development aid, its leading advocates argued that expenditure of a few hundred million dollars a year over a relatively short period would be sufficient to ensure what was then called "self-sustaining growth" in the recipient countries, so that aid could then be discontinued. Forty years and hundreds of billions of dollars later the indefinite continuation of this policy is taken for granted. Development aid has become a regular component of the budgets of Western governments, in much the same way as are defense and social services. Mr. Reginald Prentice (now Lord Prentice), when he was British minister for overseas development in the 1970s, said that aid would extend beyond the twenty-first century. This may have been a slip of the tongue. However, throughout the Western world, continuation of this policy at current or higher levels is widely seen as self-evident.

1

Indeed, wide extension of the scope of this policy of inter-governmental subsidies is already in process. Large official subsidies to the post-communist governments of the former Soviet Union and Eastern Europe have already been granted and further amounts are under discussion. Arrangements for administering and distributing these subsidies are already in place.

Within the European Community (EC), substantial and systematic transfers from governments of relatively rich countries to relatively poor ones are accepted policy, though the size of the transfers is still under debate.

Some of the proposals accepted at the 1992 United Nations Conference on the Environment (the Rio Conference) also envisage greatly expanded official transfers from the West to the third world for a variety of purposes, including protection of the environment or more effective population control.

"Foreign aid" and "development aid" are misleading expressions. To call official wealth transfers "aid" promotes an unquestioning attitude. It disarms criticism, obscures realities, and prejudges results. Who could be against aid to the less fortunate? The term has enabled aid supporters to claim a monopoly of compassion and to dismiss critics as lacking in understanding and sympathy. To paraphrase Thomas Sowell, aid is a major example of a policy that allows intellectuals and politicians to be on the side of the angels at a low apparent cost, certainly to themselves. The term also clearly implies that the policy must benefit the population of the recipient countries, which is not the case. If these transfers were generally known as government-to-government subsidies or subventions, terminology would encourage more systematic assessment.

Unfortunately, the term "development aid" is now so widely used that it is not possible to avoid it. I shall use interchangeably the terms transfers, subsidies, and aid, and occasionally refer to aid-recipient countries. It should always be remembered that most of official aid goes to governments, not to the poor, destitute, or starving people shown in aid propaganda.

In this essay I shall be concerned with the operation of these subsidies from the West to third world countries. Most of the argument also applies to Western subsidies to the post-communist governments of the former Soviet Union and Eastern Europe, to the transfers from the richer to the poorer states of the EC, and to the various subsidies envisaged by the Rio Conference.

Forty years of experience with this policy, together with some basic economic analysis and some familiarity with the cultural and political scene in recipient countries, make possible the assessment of the merits, shortcomings, and wider repercussions of this policy.

An unquestioning attitude prevails widely in public discussion of this policy. Discussions on this subject in legislatures, especially in Europe, are not debates but are akin to seminars of like-minded aid supporters or enthusiasts. Virtually the only criticism of aid in discussions in parliaments or outside is that particular governments or the West as a whole do not provide enough.

An example of this unquestioning attitude was the observation by Professor Hollis B. Chenery, full professor of economics at Harvard and formerly vice president in charge of economic research at the World Bank: "Foreign Aid is the central component of world development."[2] This statement is patently without substance. In reality, large-scale development takes place in many parts of the world without development aid, as it did long before the emergence of this policy after World War II. The prevailing unquestioning attitude has inhibited systematic examination of the potentialities, limitations, and results of these subsidies. It has also permitted conspicuous anomalies to flourish, from specific episodes to wide-ranging and prolonged policies.

The uncritical attitude to official aid has also precluded effective consideration of reforms that would direct the policy closer to its declared objectives than has so far been the case, notably to the promotion of the welfare of the peoples of the recipient countries. I shall suggest some possible reforms along these lines at a later stage in this essay.

It would be tiresome to collect and collate statistics on the diverse and large amounts of aid envisaged, committed, and dispersed in recent years by Western donors—including the international organizations and Japan—as grants and soft loans, in cash and kind, or as government guarantees of bank loans, to Eastern Europe, third world countries, and the poorer countries of the European Community. Moreover, as we shall see shortly, budgetary spending by the donors does not register some of the more important repercussions of these subsidies. What is relevant for the purpose of this essay is the certainty that the policy of large-scale official intergovernmental subsidies known as foreign aid or development aid will continue—on at least the scale of recent years.

Some Conspicuous Anomalies

I have already referred to the uncritical, unquestioning acceptance of development aid. The depth of this attitude and its consequences can be illustrated by some episodes both tragic and bizarre.

In June 1982, at the height of the Falklands War, the British government openly supplied aid to the Argentine government under a UN program, even though Argentina was using expensive and sophisticated weaponry, including Exocet missiles, against British forces. Nevertheless, this aid did not evoke any perceptible protest.

The government of Iraq, which enjoyed huge oil revenues in the 1980s, also received many millions of dollars of Western aid annually throughout this period, which facilitated the buildup of its huge military arsenal.

The extremely harsh treatment of long-serving political prisoners by the Ethiopian government, a recipient of British aid, was the subject of much protest in the 1980s. In April 1986, a British government spokesman in Parliament said that the government was doing everything possible to secure an improvement, regrettably to no avail. The suspension of official aid was, however, not envisaged.

Wider anomalies have included Western aid in the late 1970s to governments of the rich members of the Organization of Petroleum-Exporting Countries, including even Kuwait and Saudi Arabia— although the large financial surpluses of the OPEC countries were the subject of regular political and press comment, and although the Libyan government, one of the recipients, had expropriated British assets. When the OPEC countries first received Western aid they were far less rich than they became subsequently; however, the subsidies continued under their own momentum.

In the late 1970s and early 1980s, Western aid regularly went to Vietnam, while that country's government persecuted millions of its own people. Large numbers fled this persecution and descended on other aid-recipient countries in South East Asia, where their influx inflicted heavy costs on local governments and provoked political tension and conflict. In 1981, a UN fund was set up to help African refugees who had fled from governments that continued to receive Western aid.

Western aid has also often been given simultaneously to governments at war with each other, for example, India and Pakistan, Iran and Iraq, Uganda and Tanzania. This has enabled articulate anti-Westerners on both sides to claim that the West subsidizes their enemies.

There are rich people in many aid-recipient countries where there is little or no domestic income redistribution. Enterprises and individuals from such countries often buy large stakes in Western companies. In the 1980s, Nigerians were significant operators at the top end of the real estate market in London. Some London real estate agents have sent representatives to Nigeria to promote this activity. The Nigerian government had by the 1980s received substantial Western subsidies for many years. Recipient governments also often subsidize prosperous local economic interests. In Mexico the retail price of gasoline was for many years set by the government far below what it was in Western Europe and less than one-third of the price in Britain, a major aid donor to the third world.

Practically since its inception, Western aid has gone to governments hostile to the donors, whom they embarrass and thwart whenever they can. Examples range from Nkrumah's Ghana in the 1950s to Nyerere's Tanzania and Mengistu's Ethiopia in the 1980s. Many governments, especially in Africa, have received their subsidies from the West but their ideology from the communist world.

The recipients often snub the donors openly, in a humiliating fashion, without this affecting the flow of these subsidies. As recently as February 1991, Mrs. Linda Chalker (now Baroness Chalker), the British minister for overseas development, stated publicly that on a recent visit to East Africa she could not meet with representatives of the Sudanese government because no one was prepared to see her. She also said that the Sudanese government had not replied to a request for a discussion on famine in that country. She added, however, that official British aid would be extended because, ''the Government may not want it, but the people who are starving do."[3] She omitted to note that this aid went to the government, not to the starving people.

Official subsidies have at times gone specifically for the expansion in recipient countries of certain facilities, such as steel and petrochemical complexes, even when in the donor countries excess capacity in these industries was being dismantled.

Aid without Strings?

One persistent anomaly of these subsidies has been especially damaging to the peoples in the recipient countries. This has been the maintenance or expansion of subsidies in the face of the recipient governments' damaging or destructive policies.

Third world spokesmen have persistently urged at the UN and elsewhere that aid donors must not question the policies of the recipients. Such demands are evidently unreasonable since government policies directly affect the level of income and the rate of progress in recipient countries.

In fact, however, the Western donors have acted in accordance with these demands. They have continued and often increased the subsidies when the recipients pursued policies extremely damaging to their own subjects, including the poorest among them.

The long list of such policies includes persecution of the most productive groups, especially ethnic minorities, and sometimes their expulsion; suppression of trade, and at times destruction of the trading system; restriction on the inflow of foreign capital and enterprises; extensive confiscation of property, including forced collectivization; voluntary or enforced purchase of foreign enterprises, which absorbs scarce capital and deprives the country of valuable skills; price policies that discourage agricultural production; expensive forms of support of unviable activities and projects, including subsidized import substitution; and the imposition of economic controls that, among their other adverse effects, restrict external contacts and domestic mobility and so retard the spread of new ideas and methods. Many aid recipients regularly pursue several of these policies; the Ethiopian government under Mengistu pursued all of them. Western subsidies continued or increased while these policies were pursued.

Some of these consequences derive from an underlying anomaly. From their inception, the subsidies have been geared largely to the low per capita incomes in the recipient countries and occasionally also to their balance-of-payments difficulties. Major components of Western aid, such as British aid and funds distributed by IDA (the International Development Association, a World Bank affiliate), are targeted primarily toward governments of countries with very low per capita income. To support rulers on the criterion of the poverty of their subjects does nothing to discourage policies of impoverishment or even (if I may use a Marxist term) immiserization, and may even encourage them.

Many aid-recipient governments have persecuted and even expelled some of the most productive groups, including Chinese in South East Asia, or Asians and Europeans in Africa. On the criterion of poverty, such governments qualify for larger subsidies, because incomes in their countries are now reduced. A similar situation exists when a government restricts the employment opportunities of women in the name of Islamic fundamentalism.

Adoption of per capita income as the basis of aid involves another anomaly that is less evident. In discussions of aid and its allocation, per capita income in less-developed countries (LDCs) is often presented to the nearest percentage point or even fraction of one percent. In reality, as Professor Dan Usher established conclusively decades ago, these estimates are subject to errors of several hundred percent.[4] Professor Usher's findings and conclusions have been confirmed and endorsed by other prominent scholars, including Professor Paul A. Samuelson.[5]

The misleading character of the conventional national income statistics of LDCs is compounded by the inadequacy of demographic statistics. In many of these countries there is no registration of births and deaths, and in many others the registration is only rudimentary or nominal.

Large-scale spending by aid recipients on armaments is familiar, though its extent is less so. In 1981 (at the height of the so-called Cold War arms race between the superpowers), the Ministry of Economic Cooperation of the Federal Republic of Germany (the "aid ministry") estimated that third world governments then accounted for about one-fifth of total world spending on armaments. This spending by recipients was largely on arms intended for use either against their own subjects or against other aid recipients.

Lavish expenditure on obvious prestige projects by aid recipients is familiar throughout the less-developed world. It includes construction from scratch of brand-new capitals such as Brasília and Dodoma (in Tanzania), and the operation of international airlines in countries such as Burundi and Laos where the vast majority of people do not use them and local people cannot operate them. Many of these projects and enterprises, facilitated by external subsidies, represent a drain on domestic resources and have to be subsidized by local taxpayers.

Severe import restrictions in donor countries against exports from the recipient of the largess is another familiar paradox or anomaly. It is explained by the presence of influential lobbies for these subsidies in both donor and recipient countries, and similar lobbies behind the import restrictions in the donor countries. There is no effective lobby for freer trade. These restrictions, often introduced or increased at very short notice, damage the economic position and prospects of LDCs.

The flow of subsidies facilitates the maintenance of these import restrictions. Recipient governments are often loath to protest against them. They may not want to offend the influential interest groups in the donor countries, either those behind the import restrictions or those behind the subsidies, lest this jeopardize the subsidies. Instead, recipient governments often use the presence of these restrictions as an argument for further or larger transfers. Such subsidies benefit the recipient government directly, while the benefit from freer trade would accrue to the population at large.

Any public protest in the donor countries is dampened by the feeling that, by providing aid, the donor is already doing enough for the recipient, and is justified to avoid the dislocation that would be caused by the reduction of import restrictions. In this way the subsidies partake of the character of "conscience money" for the trade barriers so damaging to LDCs.

Arguments and Rationalizations

The process by which the case for official aid has come to be regarded as self-evident has been gradual. From about the 1950s to about the 1970s advocates of this policy often still found it necessary to put forward arguments or rationalizations, some of which still frequently surface in discussions on this subject.

Much the most persistent argument for these subsidies has always been that without external donations poor countries cannot emerge from poverty. Since the late 1970s another argument has become prominent, namely that the subsidies are required to improve the condition of the poorest LDCs.

Continued poverty, amounting to destitution and misery in LDCs, in contrast to the prosperity and progress in the industrialized countries, is said to be morally intolerable. Moreover the progress of the LDCs is said to be of critical political and economic importance to the West. According to this argument, without such progress, anti-Western governments would emerge in these countries, threatening Western security. Their progress, it is argued, would also provide export markets required to maintain output and employment in the West. These subsidies are therefore said to be simultaneously a moral, political, and economic imperative.

Subsidies are deemed indispensable for the progress of poor countries because such countries cannot themselves generate the capital required for their advance. This argument, popularized as the ''vicious circle'' of poverty and stagnation, was the central theme of development economics from the 1940s to the 1970s. It is still often heard, notably in the context of official assistance to post-communist governments. It was endorsed by several Nobel laureates, including Gunnar Myrdal and Paul A. Samuelson. The latter formulated it concisely: ''They [the backward nations] cannot get their heads above water because their production is so low that they can spare nothing for capital formation by which the standard of living could be raised.''[6]

In reality, throughout the world and throughout history, countless individuals, families, groups, communities, and countries have emerged from poverty to prosperity without donations, and often did so within a few years or decades. Immigrant communities in South East Asia and North America are familiar examples. The hypothesis of the vicious circle is also disproved by the existence of developed countries, all of which started poor and developed without subsidies. God did not create the world in two parts, one developed, the other undeveloped. External donations have never been necessary for the development of any society, anywhere. Indeed, as the world is a closed system that has not received resources from outside, the hypothesis is inconsistent with development as such. If it were valid, we would still be in the Old Stone Age.

Recent examples of emergence from backwardness and poverty in a few decades without subsidies are readily observable in what is nowadays called the third world. Beginning in about the 1860s, large parts of the underdeveloped world, such as South East Asia, West Africa, and Latin America, were transformed in a few decades without subsidies.

There is a distinct model behind the hypothesis of the vicious circle: the growth of income depends on investment; investment depends on saving; saving depends on income. The model pivots on the notion that the low level of income itself prevents the investment required to raise it; hence a zero or negligible rate of economic growth.

The model is refuted by obvious reality. If a hypothesis conflicts with empirical evidence, especially if it does so conspicuously, as in this case, this means either that the variables specified are unimportant, or that they do not interact in the manner postulated. Both these defects apply in this instance.

The volume of investable funds is not a critical independent determinant of economic advance. If it were, millions of people could not have advanced from poverty to prosperity within a short time.

Much research by leading scholars, including Nobel laureate Simon Kuznets, has confirmed that capital formation was a minor factor in the progress of the West since the eighteenth century, a period particularly congenial to productive investment. These findings, moreover, refer to capital formation and not simply to the volume of investable funds. It is amply clear from the experience both of communist countries and of the underdeveloped world that much spending termed ''investment'' does not result in assets yielding a net flow of valuable goods and services.

Poor people can generate or secure sufficient funds to start themselves on the road to progress, if they are motivated to improve their material condition and are not inhibited by government policy or lack of public security. They can save modest amounts even from small incomes to make possible direct investment in agriculture, trading, the purchase of simple tools and equipment, and many other purposes. They can work harder or longer, or they can redeploy their activities more productively—for instance, by replacing subsistence crops by cash crops or producing both simultaneously.

Moreover, governments and enterprises of poor countries have access to commercial external funds. For instance, in black Africa European merchants routinely lend to their trustworthy African customers, mostly traders; indeed, such lending is virtually a condition of doing business there. The traders in turn lend to farmers or to smaller traders. Much the same applies in South and South East Asia. LDC governments can readily borrow abroad, perhaps too readily. It is evident that ability to borrow abroad does not depend on the level of income but on responsible conduct and the capacity to use funds productively. All this applied also in Eastern Europe before World War II.

If property rights are clearly defined and reasonably protected, external commercial funds are available, even in the face both of poverty and of pronounced political risk. Since World War II much foreign investment has taken place in Asia and Africa amid great political uncertainty, as it does now to some extent in Eastern Europe and the former Soviet Union.

Thus, subsidies from abroad are plainly not necessary for emergence from backwardness and poverty. It is indeed unwarranted and distasteful condescension to argue that the peoples of Eastern Europe or the third world, unlike those of the West, cannot achieve material progress without donations from abroad.

Development aid, far from being necessary to rescue poor societies from a vicious circle of poverty, is far more likely to keep them in that state. It promotes dependence on others. It encourages the idea that emergence from poverty depends on external donations rather than on people's own efforts, motivation, arrangements, and institutions.

In reality, official development aid creates a vicious circle. Poverty is instanced as ground for aid; aid creates dependence and thus keeps people in poverty. Emergence from poverty requires effort, firmly established property rights, and productive investment.

The arguments that the subsidies necessary for the advance of the recipients also benefit the donors are invalid also. The emergence of an anti-Western government does not depend on the level of a country's income or on its rate of change, as is clear throughout the less-developed world. For instance, articulate hostility to the West, and especially to the United States, in areas such as the Muslim Middle East or in Latin America, is in no way related to income.

It is also inconsistent to argue that aid-recipient LDCs said to be acutely or desperately short of resources could present a serious political or security threat to the donors. This is evident in considering particular third world countries. It applies also to the third world as a whole, which is a highly diverse collectivity of frequently antagonistic constituents. They act together only within international organizations or through them, and this collaboration, including these organizations and venues, is usually financed by the West.

The notion that the economies of the donors benefit from the subsidies simply ignores the cost of the resources given away. Enterprises do not prosper by giving away money, even if the recipients use some or all of the funds to buy the products of those enterprises.

Such subventions are also not sufficient for economic advance. The many billions of dollars' worth of official aid over the years to Ethiopia, Sudan, and many other African countries have not secured their progress. In history, the huge inflow of precious metals into Spain from America (perhaps the greatest windfall received by any country before the twentieth century) did not prevent the relative economic decline of Spain compared to, say, Britain and the Netherlands in the sixteenth and seventeenth centuries. Such sequences are not surprising. With few exceptions, irrelevant in our context—such as inherited private wealth or windfalls—the possession of money is the result of economic achievement, not its precondition.

I may mention in passing that the principal argument for subsidies to the reformist post-communist governments is much the same as the plainly invalid core argument for subsidies to third world governments. The old clichés have also been taken out of mothballs, such as those claiming that subsidies help people to help themselves, or that they act as a catalyst for private investment.

What Can Subsidies Achieve?

External donations are thus evidently neither necessary nor sufficient for the emergence from poverty of poor countries. This still leaves open the question whether they promote or retard economic advance. It may seem plausible, indeed self-evident, that they must be helpful to advance. As they represent an inflow of subsidized resources, it may appear that they must improve economic conditions and prospects. However, this does not follow.

The inflow of subsidies sets up various adverse repercussions that can far outweigh any benefits and are indeed likely to do so. Some of these repercussions arise whether the subventions go to a country's private sector or to its government, others because they go to the government.

To begin with a somewhat technical point: external subsidies raise the real rate of exchange in the receiving country and thereby impair foreign trade competitiveness. This effect can be offset or outweighed to the extent that the subsidies enhance the overall productivity of resources, as is the usual result of an inflow of private capital, especially equity capital expected to yield a commercial return. Such an increase in productivity is much less likely with official subsidies, as these are rarely expected to produce a positive real return. Moreover, any increase in productivity can occur only after a time lag of years, over which period the higher real exchange rate makes for continued dependence on external assistance.

Subventions from abroad promote or reinforce the belief that economic improvement depends on outside forces rather than domestic effort. The prospect of subsidies encourages governments to seek them through beggary or blackmail, rather than to consider the potentialities of change at home. Such attitudes and conduct can spread from the government to other sectors of the population.

Unlike manna from heaven, which descends indiscriminately on the whole population, these subsidies go to the governments. Although in some instances subsidies go through governments rather than to them, in our context the distinction is immaterial, because the direction and use of the funds require government approval in the recipient countries. They therefore increase the resources, patronage, and power of the government, compared with that of the rest of society. External subsidies have also helped to sustain governments whose policies have proved so damaging that only the subsidies have enabled them to remain in power and continue on their destructive course. Altogether, the subsidies have contributed significantly to the politicization of life in the third world since World War II.[7] When economic or social life is extensively politicized, people's fortunes come to depend on government policy and administrative decisions. The stakes, both gains and losses, in the struggle for power, increase greatly. These circumstances encourage or even force people to divert attention, energy, and resources from productive economic activity to concern with the outcome of political and administrative decisions; and the deployment of people's energy and resources necessarily affects the economic performance of any society.

Politicization of life often provokes tension and conflict, especially in countries with heterogenous ethnic and cultural groups, including much of the third world and Eastern Europe. Extensive politicization of life has been a major factor behind the ubiquitous conflicts, often armed, on the contemporary scene. In Asia and Africa, groups and communities that have lived together peaceably for generations have been set against each other by the politicization promoted by these official subsidies; for instance, in Lebanon, Christians and Muslims; in Malaysia, Malays and Chinese; in Sri Lanka, Singhalese and Tamils; and, in Nigeria, Ibo and Hausa.

The subsidies also make it easier for governments to restrict the inflow of foreign commercial capital, especially equity capital. Third world governments usually pay lip service to inward foreign equity investment, but in practice many severely restrict it. They do so because these restrictions suit their political purposes and the commercial interests of their supporters. The inflow of subsidies makes it easier for them to restrict foreign commercial investment, notably equity investment.

These restrictions are plainly anomalous when shortage of capital is used as the basic argument for the subsidies. Inflow of equity capital, together with the commercial, administrative, and technical skills that accompany it, have been the prime instrument of the economic advance of many LDCs. The restrictions are therefore correspondingly damaging.

A Double Asymmetry

As we have seen, external subsidies are neither necessary nor sufficient for economic advance. Whether they promote or inhibit it cannot be established conclusively. As commercial capital from abroad is available to people who can use it productively, it follows that the maximum contribution of external subsidies to economic advance cannot exceed the avoided cost of borrowing—that is, interest and amortization charges as the proportion of national income that would have been payable to the lenders. The most the subsidies can do is to reduce the cost of a resource, which is not a major factor in economic advance. Except possibly for very small economies, this benefit is far too small to affect the national income appreciably.

It is of much practical significance to recognize that the inflow of subsidies entails major adverse repercussions, especially by promoting the politicization of life, with disastrous effects in much of the third world. The belief that an inflow of resources must benefit the population at large has helped along the uncritical acceptance of development aid. After all, it is thought that the West can readily afford to give away a few billion dollars a year, as this may do some good and cannot harm the population of the recipient countries, so that even if the funds are wasted no great harm results. If the damaging repercussions are recognized, a more questioning stance toward these subsidies might come to be adopted by people, including genuinely compassionate people.

In the operation of these subsidies there is a double asymmetry in their effects on economic advance. The first asymmetry is the following: any favorable effect through the reduction in the cost of investable resources is a saving on a resource that is not critical for development. Major adverse effects, on the other hand, operate on critical determinants, namely political and social determinants, and to some extent also on foreign trade and competitiveness.

The second asymmetry is that a volume of subsidies too small to benefit economic performance appreciably is, nevertheless, amply sufficient to bring about adverse effects. It is the relationship of the subsidies to national income that is relevant to the favorable effect, namely a reduction in the cost of investable funds. Because subsidies go to governments, it is the relationship of the subsidies to government receipts and foreign exchange earnings (themselves readily subject to government control) that is relevant to major adverse repercussions. Because national income is necessarily a multiple of tax receipts, generally a large multiple in less-developed countries, the subsidies are necessarily far larger relative to tax receipts and foreign exchange earnings than they are to national income.

Economic performance and progress of entire societies are components of historical development that depends on literally countless past and present factors operating with different and varying time lags, many of them outside the scope of economic analysis. Assessment of the overall result of such subsidies must depend also on assumptions about official policies that would have been pursued in their absence. It is not surprising that attempts to evaluate the contribution of external subsidies to overall development by means of correlation analysis have yielded widely different or conflicting results, even when undertaken by committed aid supporters. It is therefore necessary to rely on certain general considerations, supplemented by specific instances of empirical evidence. That is the procedure adopted here, a procedure that results in a distinct, but not conclusive, presumption that external subsidies are more likely to inhibit economic advance than to promote it.

These uncertainties in no way affect the conclusion that the contribution to development of these subsidies cannot exceed the avoided cost of borrowing, and that this contribution must be very modest and can be easily offset or outweighed by the adverse repercussions of the inflow of subsidies.

Aid and Poverty

The argument for these subsidies most widely voiced since the early 1980s has been that they improve the lot of the poorest people in LDCs. This argument is misdirected. The subsidies do not go to the pathetic figures pictured in aid propaganda. They go to their rulers, who are often directly responsible for the harsh condition of their subjects. Even when this is not so, it is still the case that the condition of the poorest is very low among the priorities of aid recipients, as is evident from their policies, including the patterns of government spending.

When third world governments refer to the need for redistribution they usually mean increased subsidies from the West. In their own countries they are apt to interpret redistribution as confiscation of the assets of politically unpopular and vulnerable groups, and those of their political opponents.

In most of the third world there is no machinery for state relief of acute poverty and need. Thus, even if a recipient government wanted to use aid to help the poorest, this can be difficult, even impossible. What is more important, such help may not accord with the political or personal interests or ideological priorities of third world rulers, or indeed with local mores. In fact, it often conflicts with these priorities and mores. This situation is evident in multiracial, multitribal or multicultural countries. An Arab-dominated Sudanese government will not help the poorest blacks in southern Sudan, hundreds of miles away, with whom it is in persistent armed conflict. The rulers of Ethiopia will not help the people of Tigre, whose distress is caused or exacerbated by the military action of the government. In Sri Lanka a Singhalese-dominated government is unlikely to help the Tamil poor. Such examples can be readily multiplied.

In the context of aid for development I have already recited a long list of policies that affect development adversely. These policies also exacerbate acute poverty.

In many aid-recipient countries it is the poorest who are worst hit by policies such as enforced population transfers, suppression of trade, and forced collectivization, and also by the civil wars and other forms of breakdown of public security. These policies and conditions have forced large numbers of people to rely for their existence on precarious subsistence agriculture, the hazards of which have become particularly plain in Africa.

Indeed, as we have seen, the criterion of the allocation of much Western aid does nothing to discourage policies of impoverishment or immiserization, and is in fact more likely to reward them. Thus, the more damaging the policies, the more acute becomes the need, the more effective become appeals for aid. The experience of Ethiopia and the Sudan in the 1980s makes this clear. The destructive policies of these governments have been largely responsible for the mass misery that in turn has been so effective in eliciting large sums both of official aid and private charity.

Although government-to-government subsidies can do little or nothing, either for economic development or for relief of the worst poverty, they can alleviate acute shortages, especially of imports. By maintaining a minimum level of consumption, the subsidies avert total collapse and conceal from the population, at least temporarily, the worst effects of destructive policies. External subsidies also suggest extended endorsement of these policies. These results in turn help the government to remain in power and to persist in its policies without provoking popular revolt. This result of external donations has been conspicuous in such African countries as Ethiopia, Sudan, Tanzania, and Uganda.

The role of external subsidies in alleviating an acute shortage of consumer goods, especially of imports, is pertinent to the extension of this policy to post-communist governments. Reformist governments in Eastern Europe and in the constituent republics of the former Soviet Union face formidable obstacles resulting from the legacy of decades or generations of totalitarian command economies. Attempted reforms engender popular discontent, which is exacerbated by shortage of consumer goods including necessities. In such conditions, subsidies having a firmly limited period of operation and linked to the pursuit of reformist policies may be helpful or even necessary for the survival of the reformers. This, in turn, may serve the humanitarian and political interests of Western donors.

Why the Unquestioning Attitude?

It is not clear why the case for these subsidies has come to be taken as practically self-evident. Reflection on the reasons behind people's stances toward an argument or policy cannot be conclusive, and such reflections can never decide the validity of an argument or the assessment of a policy. The validity of an argument depends on its logical consistency and conformity with empirical evidence. Assessment of a policy depends partly on value judgments, partly on the relation between the outcome of the policy and its proclaimed purposes, and partly on conjecture about other policies that might have been pursued.

Nevertheless, the unquestioning attitude toward a policy that has produced startling anomalies and damaging results invites some speculation about the factors or forces that have inhibited, and still inhibit, systematic and critical examination. Clearly there is a need for a more questioning attitude. Indeed, the need is now even greater than ever, in view of the extension of this policy to Eastern Europe and the former Soviet Union.

The factors behind the unquestioning attitude may include the acceptance of the term ''aid'' for these subsidies, the practice of identifying the interests of recipient rulers with those of the population at large, the belief that the subsidies cannot damage the interests of people in the recipient countries, and feelings of guilt in the West about its own prosperity.

It is unlikely, however, that these influences by themselves would have sufficed to sustain the unquestioning attitude in the face of startling anomalies. A more likely explanation is that the influences just recited have been supported by the operation of powerful and articulate political, administrative, and commercial interests. These groups include the national and international aid organizations and bureaucracies, notably the United Nations and its offshoots, including its regional commissions in Asia, Africa, and Latin America; the World Bank; the International Monetary Fund; churches and other aid lobbies; and the commercial beneficiaries of aid transfers.

A further reason, of interest primarily to academics, may be the acceptance in development economics of modern macroeconomic theory, including unrefined Keynesian methodology, without recognition of its limitations.

Here is a rarely quoted but key passage from Keynes's *The General Theory:* ''We take as given the existing skill and quantity of available labour, the existing quality and quantity of available equipment, the existing technique, the degree of competition, the tastes and habits of the consumer, the disutility of different intensities of labour and of the activities of supervision and organization, as well as the social structure.''[8]

It is debatable whether acceptance of such assumptions is helpful for the analysis of fluctuations in output and employment in advanced industrial economies. It is plainly inappropriate for an examination of the factors behind the economic performance and advance of entire societies. For this purpose, acceptance of these assumptions deprives the analysis of all explanatory power. The factors taken as given in the Keynesian analysis and in other models built on it, prominent in academic and public discussion of development, take as given critical cultural, political, and social determinants of economic achievement and progress. These determinants, moreover, usually interact with the familiar variables of economic analysis.

Reform of Aid

Official subsidies ought to be terminated. This seems impractical, partly because of the momentum of existing commitments, partly because of the extremely powerful and articulate interest groups behind the policy. But there are certain reforms that, if implemented, could bring the operation of these transfers closer to their proclaimed objectives.

The most important single reform would be a radical change in the criteria of allocation. These subsidies should go to those governments whose policies are most likely to promote the economic progress and general welfare of their peoples through humane leadership, effective administration, and the extension of personal freedom. Such a reform would remove the most conspicuous anomalies of official aid and enable it to make whatever contribution it can to improve the condition and prospects of the poorest.

This proposal differs altogether from suggestions to link further aid to the adoption of more market-oriented policies by the recipients. Such suggestions are unlikely to be implemented in practice. Extensive state control implies concentration of power, the exercise of patronage, and conferment of privileges. Such a situation suits the purposes of most aid-recipient governments. They are likely to abandon it only if its continued pursuit would threaten an economic breakdown endangering their position. Otherwise, they are unlikely to do more than pay lip service to the market, combined perhaps with some changes in macroeconomic financial policies (including foreign exchange policies) and some largely cosmetic changes in other directions.

To subsidize governments before they have clearly abandoned policies that suit their interests makes it easier for them to continue existing policies. As U.S. Senator Strom Thurmond has said, "you cannot get a hog to butcher itself."

Official subsidies should be bilateral, not multilateral—which would permit some control by the elected representatives of the taxpayers who are the real donors. Moreover, under the bilateral system there is somewhat closer contact between the suppliers and the users of the funds, which promotes their more effective use. It is also easier to discontinue bilateral subsidies in the face of patently destructive and barbarous policies.

To serve the proclaimed purposes of development aid, the subsidies ought to be "untied" (that is, separated from purchases of exports from particular donors). Subsidies to third world governments could then be distinguished from support of exporters and their bankers in the donor countries.

The subsidies ought to take the form of straightforward grants rather than subsidized loans. Such loans confuse donations with investment and set up tensions between donors and recipients. Moreover, when tied aid and subsidized loans are linked, as they often are in practice, it becomes quite impossible to ascertain who gets how much and from whom; that is, whether and to what extent the taxpayers of the donor countries subsidize the aid-recipient governments, rather than various interests in their own countries.

Such proposals for reform may be worth reciting, but they are unlikely to be implemented. That is so not only because the policy of development aid is supported by powerful interests, but also because existing methods and practices benefit such groups, notably exporters of goods and services.

There is therefore little prospect in the foreseeable future of substantial reform of the procedures and practices of official aid, including the methods of allocation. These are likely to persist in the extension of subsidies to the governments of Eastern Europe and the former Soviet Union.

NOTES

1. In accordance with standard practice, throughout this essay "aid" refers to official economic aid; that is, subsidies from donor governments to recipient governments both directly and indirectly, through international organizations. It includes the grant element in soft loans. It excludes military aid, private investment, and the activities of charities. The West includes Western Europe, the United States, Canada, Japan, Australia, and New Zealand; that is, it refers to the members of the Organization for Economic Cooperation and Development.

2. *The New York Times,* March 1, 1981.

3. *The Times* (London), February 6, 1991.

4. Professor Usher wrote more than twenty years ago: "Statistics like these may contain errors of several hundred per cent . . . the discrepancy is not due primarily to errors in data . . . the fault lies with the rules [of national income comparisons] themselves . . . [which], generate numbers that fail to carry the implications expected of them." (Dan Usher, "Introduction and Summary," *The Price Mechanism and the Meaning of National Income Statistics,* Oxford, 1968.) While this book is the most comprehensive exposition of Professor Usher's findings, he published his central argument several years earlier, including his article "The Transport Bias in Comparisons of National Income," *Economica* 30, no. 118 (May 1963):140–158. He wrote there: "The conventional comparison shows that the per capita national income of the United Kingdom is about fourteen times that of Thailand. Recomputations made by the author to allow for various biases in the comparison suggest that the effective ratio of living standards is about three to one" (page 140).

5. Paul A. Samuelson, "Professor Dan Usher's Contribution to National Income Comparisons," *Economic Journal* 85, no. 339 (September 1975):614. See also I. B. Kravis, A. W. Heston, and B. Summers, "Real GDP Per Capita for More than One Hundred Countries," *Economic Journal* 88, no. 350 (June 1978):215–242.

6. Paul A. Samuelson, *Economics: An Introductory Analysis,* 2nd ed. (New York, 1951), 49.

7. Politicization of life can of course also come about through processes quite unrelated to external subsidies. These played no part in the wholesale politicization of life in Eastern Europe, which was the outcome of wars, revolutions, and intellectual influences.

8. J. M. Keynes, *The General Theory of Employment, Interest and Money* (London, 1936), 245.